Frida

Yuyi Morales

Photography by
Tim O'Meara

A NEAL PORTER BOOK
ROARING BROOK PRESS
NEW YORK

Soy
I am

Yo . . .
I . . .

busco **search**

Veo

I see

¡Aja!

Ah-ha!

Juego **I play**

Sueño
I dream

Y me doy cuenta . . .

And I realize . . .

de que . . . .
that . . .

siento
I feel

Y entiendo . . .

And I understand . . .

que amo
that
I love

Y creo arte

And create

Y por lo tanto . . .

And so . . .

¡Vivo!

I live!

My Frida Kahlo

When I think of Frida Kahlo, I think of *orgullo*, pride. Growing up in Mexico, I wanted to know more about this woman with her mustache and unibrow. Who was this artist who had unapologetically filled her paintings with old and new symbols of Mexican culture in order to tell her own story?

I wasn't always so taken by Frida. When I was younger, I often found her paintings tortuous and difficult to understand. The more I learned about Frida's life, the more her paintings began to take on new light for me. I finally saw that what had terrified me about Frida's images was actually her way of expressing the things she felt, feared, and wanted.

Frida's life was one of *muchas risas*, lots of laughs, for she loved to joke and sing and curse. Born in a blue house in Coyoacán, Mexico, in 1907, young Frida could not rein in her creativity. She was a natural storyteller who often dressed up as a boy and even had an imaginary friend. But there were also many *lágrimas*, or tears. At age six, she contracted polio, a very serious and then-common disease that left her right leg withered for the rest of her life. When she was eighteen, she was in a terrible bus accident that left her body so badly mangled that she had to endure painful medical procedures for the rest of her life. While she was lying in a hospital bed recovering, she began to paint.

It is thought that during her lifetime, Frida created 143 paintings, 55 of which were self-portraits. She would study her reflection in the mirror and paint herself wearing elaborate jewelry or crowned with enormous braids, ribbons, and flowers. She would paint herself accompanied by her pet monkey, Fulang-Chang, her dog, Xolot, her parrots, or even her husband, the famous Mexican muralist, Diego Rivera.

Sometimes she would paint her head on the body of a wounded deer. Her work was proud and unafraid and introduced the world to a side of Mexican culture that had been hidden from view.

As a child, while learning to draw, I would often study my own reflection in the mirror and think about Frida. Did she know how many artists she influenced with her courage and her ability to overcome her own limitations?

Frida died in 1954, at the age of forty-seven. Her body was frail but her spirit was indomitable and her legacy lives on. Viva Frida!

Mi Frida Kahlo

Pensar en Frida Kahlo me llena con orgullo. Durante mucho tiempo había querido saber quién era esa mujer con bigote y esas cejas unidas de lado a lado. ¿Quién era esta artista que, sin tapujos, había llenado sus pinturas con los símbolos antiguos y nuevos de la cultura mexicana en el afán de contar su propia historia?

No siempre me sentí cercana a Frida. Al crecer en México, durante mi juventud, sus pinturas me parecían tortuosas y difíciles de entender, pero mientras más aprendía de su vida esas pinturas comenzaban a iluminarse para mí. Finalmente me di cuenta que eso que me había espantado de las imágenes de Frida era tan solo la manera que ella tenía de expresar las cosas que sentía, lo que temía y lo que deseaba.

La vida de Frida estuvo llena de muchas risas, pues a ella le encantaba bromear, cantar y hasta decir palabrotas. Nacida en una casa azul en Coyoacán, México, en 1907, Frida nunca frenó su creatividad. Desde niña imaginaba cuentos, en ocasiones se vistió de hombre, y hasta tuvo una amiga imaginaria. También hubieron muchas lágrimas. A los seis años Frida contrajo polio, una fuerte enfermedad muy común en aquel entonces, y esto la dejó con la pierna derecha más delgada que la izquierda. Cuando tenía dieciocho años Frida sufrió un terrible accidente de camión que la dejó tan lastimada que, por el resto de su vida, tuvo que soportar muchos tratamientos médicos muy dolorosos. Mientras estaba en cama recuperándose fue que empezó a pintar.

Se cree que durante su vida Frida creo 143 pinturas, de las cuales 55 fueron autorretratos. Frente al espejo miraba su reflejo y se pintaba adornada de joyería fantástica, o coronada con sus enormes trenzas, listones y flores. Se pintaba acompañada de su mascota, el chango Fulang-Chang, su perro Xolot, sus pericos y hasta con su esposo, el famoso muralista mexicano Diego Rivera. Una vez pintó su cabeza en el cuerpo de un venado herido. Su trabajo era orgulloso y atrevido, reveló al mundo una visión de la cultura mexicana que hasta entonces se había mantenido escondida.

De niña, cuando estaba yo aprendiendo a dibujar, a menudo examinaba mi propio reflejo en el espejo y pensaba en Frida. ¿Sabría ella a cuantos artistas influenciaría con su valor y su habilidad para vencer sus propias limitaciones?

Frida murió en 1954 a la edad de cuarenta y siete años. Su cuerpo era frágil pero su espíritu fue indomable y su legado vivirá para siempre. ¡Viva Frida!

Yuyi

Para las aladas. For the winged ones:

Sita, Ana, Solecito, Meche, Moni, Eloina, Eli y Magy

Copyright © 2014 by Yuyi Morales

A Neal Porter Book

Published by Roaring Brook Press

Roaring Brook Press is a division of Holtzbrinck Publishing Holdings Limited Partnership

175 Fifth Avenue, New York, New York 10010

The art for this book was made with stop-motion puppets made from steel, polymer clay, and wool,

acrylic paints, photography, and digital manipulation.

mackids.com

Library of Congress Cataloging-in-Publication Data

Morales, Yuyi.

Viva Frida! / Yuyi Morales. — First edition.

    pages cm

"A Neal Porter book."

ISBN 978-1-59643-603-9 (hardcover)

1. Kahlo, Frida—Juvenile literature. 2.

Painters—Mexico—Biography—Juvenile literature. I. Title.

ND259.K33M66 2014

759.972—dc23

                                    2013044236

Roaring Brook Press books may be purchased for business or promotional use. For information

on bulk purchases please contact Macmillan Corporate and Premium Sales Department

at (800) 221-7945 x5442 or by email at specialmarkets@macmillan.com.

First edition 2014

Book design by Jennifer Browne

Printed in China by South China Printing Co. Ltd,

Dongguan City, Guangdong Province

1   3   5   7   9   10   8   6   4   2